"Just for You"

A
SPECIAL COLLECTION
OF
INSPIRATIONAL VERSES
BY

Helen Steiner Rice

DOUBLEDAY & COMPANY, INC.

GARDEN CITY, NEW YORK

ISBN: 0-385-07721-1
Library of Congress Catalog Card Number 67-10385
Copyright © 1967 by Gibson Greeting Cards, Inc.
All Rights Reserved
Printed in the United States of America
30   29   28   27

Dedication

Dedicated to Responsive Hearts
    wherever they may be,
For the love and inspiration
    they keep giving generously . . .
For the things that I have written
    do not belong to me,
They reflect the many people
    who have quite unconsciously
Inspired my life and writings
    in a myriad of ways
And encouraged all my efforts
    with their warm and generous praise . . .
So each book is a tribute
    for little daily graces
That have come to me across/the world
    from little-dreamed-of places.

HELEN STEINER RICE

About the Author

Helen Steiner Rice, to quote one columnist, "talks about God as if He were right at her elbow and she sincerely believes that He is."

It is the sheer simplicity and uncomplicated style of her verses that have appealed to people of all countries, colors and creeds. In six years of continuous writing there has never been one letter of criticism or dissent from any source.

Letters from the distinguished and the famous, as well as the unheralded housewife and the lonely shut-in, all strike a common note—"You are one of us" . . .

"I cried tears of gratitude and joy at your complete understanding of our frailties."

"Your spirit of humility is like a shining light that brightens earth's darkest spots."

"Only one who has suffered deeply and had a very close contact with God would be able to put into words the messages you have given the world."

"What gave you that special knowledge and depth to be able to reach people in such a wonderful way?"

"You could never write the lines you do except for God dwelling in you."

"If I ever meet you I will know I have seen the *face* of *God*."

"I am only a housewife and not a wealthy woman, but I feel rich indeed after reading something of yours."

A well-known columnist writing of her works said, "Her poems can be applied to almost anything an individual feels is lacking in his life . . . whether it be worldly possessions, physical endowments, or spiritual serenity. They can conjure a world of fantasy for the small child, give moral strength to the teen-ager, encouragement to the young adult, and comfort to the old. They can soothe the sick and delight the well, inspire the discouraged and appease the overly ambitious, assure the good and change the bad."

Her audience is far-flung and beyond counting. In *Gaya, India,* at the Nazareth Academy, a selfless nun uses her books in her classroom . . . in *Suginami-Ku, Tokyo,* the Murakami Bible Class reads her writings daily . . . the armed forces in *Okinawa* and the *Philippines* listen to her poems over the air . . . on a public bus in *Hong Kong,* American visitors report hearing her verses read . . . A bishop in *Australia* writes for permission to reprint her poems for his parishioners, and a publishing house in *South Africa* is translating her writings to be distributed. From *Oslo, Norway*—asking the postmaster to help find this writer—come these words: "From American friends we have got such beautiful books written by you, and they fill our hearts with joy." From *Viet Nam* a soldier writes, "A fellow soldier let me read a copy of *The Praying Hands* by Helen Steiner Rice, and to me it is the most beautiful poem I have ever read and I would like to have a copy to carry with me."

She writes not as a writer but as a friend who has known you always, and she feels that with the help of responsive hearts the whole complexion of this violent world can be changed. Through her writings she hopes that all races, colors and creeds can be brought closer to God and to each other where every *stranger* is a *friend* and every *man* a *brother*.

Contents

Foreword

Show me the way,
   not to fortune and fame,
Not how to win laure's
   or praise for my name—
But Show Me The Way
   to spread "The Great Story"
That "Thine is The Kingdom
   and Power and Glory."

HELEN STEINER RICE

We all need words to live by,
To inspire us and guide us,
Words to give us courage
When the trials of life betide us—
And the words that never fail us
Are the words of God above,
Words of comfort and of courage
Filled with wisdom and with love—
They are ageless and enduring,
They have lived through generations,
There's no question left unanswered
In our Father's revelations—
And in this ever-changing world
God's words remain unchanged,
For though through countless ages
They've been often re-arranged,
The *truth* shines through all changes
Just as *bright today* as *when*
Our Father made the *universe*
And breathed His Life in men—
And the words of inspiration
That I write for you today
Are just the old enduring truths
Said in a rhythmic way—
And if my "borrowed words of truth"
In some way touch your heart,
Then I am deeply thankful
To have had a little part
In sharing these *God-given lines,*
And I hope you'll share them, too,
With family, friends and loved ones
And all those dear to *you.*

HELEN STEINER RICE

The "Praying Hands" are much, much more
    than just a work of art,
They are the "soul's creation"
    of a deeply thankful heart—
They are a Priceless Masterpiece
    that love alone could paint,
And they reveal the Selflessness
    of an unheralded saint—
These hands so scarred and toilworn,
    tell the story of a man
Who sacrificed his talent
    in accordance with God's Plan—
For in God's Plan are many things
    man cannot understand,
But we must trust God's judgment
    and be guided by His Hand—
Sometimes He asks us to give up
    our dreams of happiness,
Sometimes we must forego our hopes
    of fortune and success,

Not all of us can triumph
  or rise to heights of fame,
And many times What Should Be Ours,
  goes to Another Name—
But he who makes a sacrifice,
  so another may succeed,
Is indeed a true disciple
  of our blessed Saviour's creed—
For when we "give ourselves away"
  in sacrifice and love,
We are "laying up rich treasures"
  in God's kingdom up above—
And hidden in gnarled, toilworn hands
  is the truest Art of Living,
Achieved alone by those who've learned
  the "Victory of Giving"—
For any sacrifice on earth
  made in the dear Lord's name,
Assures the Giver of a Place
  in Heaven's Hall of Fame—
And who can say with certainty
  Where the Greatest Talent Lies,
Or Who Will Be the Greatest
  In Our Heavenly Father's Eyes!

Just close your eyes
    and open your heart
And feel your worries
    and cares depart,
Just yield yourself
    to the Father above
And let Him hold you
    secure in His love—
For life on earth
    grows more involved
With endless problems
    that can't be solved—
But God only asks us
    to do our best,
Then He will "take over"
    and finish the rest—
So when you are tired,
    discouraged and blue,

There's always one door
    that is open to you—
And that is the door
    to "The House of Prayer"
And you'll find God waiting
    to meet you there,
And "The House of Prayer"
    is no farther away
Than the quiet spot
    where you kneel and pray—
For the heart is a temple
    when God is there
As we place ourselves
    in His loving care,
And He hears every prayer
    and answers each one
When we pray in His name
    "Thy Will be done"—
And the burdens that seemed
    too heavy to bear
Are lifted away
    on *"the wings of prayer."*

I've never seen God,
        but I know how I feel,
It's people like *you*
        who make Him *"so real"* . . .
My God is no stranger,
        He's friendly and gay
And He doesn't ask me
        to weep when I pray . . .
It seems that I pass Him
        so often each day
In the faces of people
        I meet on my way . . .
He's the stars in the heaven,
        a smile on some face,
A leaf on a tree
        or a rose in a vase . . .
He's winter and autumn
        and summer and spring,
In short, *God is every*
        real, wonderful thing . . .
I wish I might meet Him
        much more than I do,
I would if there were
        more people like you.

"The earth is the Lord's
   and the fulness thereof"—
It speaks of His greatness,
   it sings of His love,
And each day at dawning
   I lift my heart high
And raise up my eyes
   to the infinite sky . . .
I watch the night vanish
   as a new day is born,
And I hear the birds sing
   on the wings of the morn,
I see the dew glisten
   in crystal-like splendor
While God, with a touch
   that is gentle and tender,
Wraps up the night
   and softly tucks it away
And hangs out the sun
   to herald a new day . . .
And so I give thanks
   and my heart kneels to pray—
"*God*, keep me and guide me
   and go with me today."

The End of the Road
Is but a Bend in the Road

When we feel we have nothing left to give
And we are sure that the "song has ended"—
When our day seems over and the shadows fall
And the darkness of night has descended,
Where can we go to find the strength
To valiantly keep on trying,
Where can we find the hand that will dry
The tears that the heart is crying—
There's but one place to go and that is to God
And, dropping all pretense and pride,
We can pour out our problems without restraint
And gain strength with Him at our side—
And together we stand at life's crossroads
And view what we think is the end,
But God has a much bigger vision
And He tells us it's *only a bend*—
For the road goes on and is smoother,
And the "pause in the song" is a "rest,"
And the part that's unsung and unfinished
Is the sweetest and richest and best—
So rest and relax and grow stronger,
Let go and *let God* share your load,
Your work is not finished or ended,
You've just come to "*a bend in the road.*"

God Knows Best

Our Father knows what's best for us,
So why should we complain—
We always want the sunshine,
But He knows there must be rain—
We love the sound of laughter
And the merriment of cheer,
But our hearts would lose their tenderness
If we never shed a tear . . .
Our Father tests us often
With suffering and with sorrow,
He tests us, not to punish us,
But to help us meet *tomorrow* . . .
For growing trees are strengthened
When they withstand the storm,
And the sharp cut of the chisel
Gives the marble grace and form . . .
God never hurts us needlessly,
And He never wastes our pain
For every loss He sends to us
Is followed by rich gain . . .
And when we count the blessings
That God has so freely sent,
We will find no cause for murmuring
And no time to lament . . .
For our Father loves His children,
And to Him all things are plain,
So He never sends us *pleasure*
When the *soul's deep need is pain* . . .
So whenever we are troubled,
And when everything goes wrong,
It is just God working in us
To make *our spirit strong.*

The legend of the raindrop
Has a lesson for us all
As it trembled in the heavens . . .
Questioning whether it should fall—
For the glistening raindrop argued
To the genie of the sky
"I am beautiful and lovely
As I sparkle here on high,
And hanging here I will become
Part of the rainbow's hue
And I'll shimmer like a diamond
For all the world to view" . . .
But the genie told the raindrop,
"Do not hesitate to go,
For you will be more beautiful
If you fall to earth below,
For you will sink into the soil
And be lost a while from sight,

But when you reappear on earth,
You'll be looked on with delight;
For you will be the raindrop
That quenched the thirsty ground
And helped the lovely flowers
To blossom all around,
And in your resurrection
You'll appear in queenly clothes
With the beauty of the lily
And the fragrance of the rose;
Then, when you wilt and wither,
You'll become part of the earth
And make the soil more fertile
And give new flowers birth" . . .
For there is nothing ever lost
Or *eternally neglected*,
For *everything God ever made*
Is always resurrected;
So trust God's all-wise wisdom
And doubt the Father never,
For in *His Heavenly Kingdom*
There is nothing lost forever.

A very favorite story of mine
Is about *two seas* in *Palestine*

One is a sparkling sapphire jewel,
Its waters are clean and clear and cool,
Along its shores the children play
And travelers seek it on their way,
And *Nature* gives so lavishly
Her choicest gems to the *Galilee:*

But on to the south the Jordan flows
Into a sea where nothing grows,
No splash of fish, no singing bird,
No children's laughter is ever heard,
The air hangs heavy all around
And *Nature* shuns this barren ground:

Both seas receive the Jordan's flow,
The water is just the same, we know,
But one of the seas, like liquid sun,

Can warm the hearts of everyone,
While farther south another sea
Is dead and dark and miserly—
It takes each drop the Jordan brings
And to each drop it fiercely clings,
It hoards and holds the Jordan's waves
Until like shackled, captured slaves
The fresh, clear Jordan turns to salt
And dies within the *Dead Sea's* vault:

But the Jordan flows on rapturously
As it enters and leaves the *Galilee,*
For every drop that the Jordan gives
Becomes a laughing wave that lives—
For the *Galilee* gives back each drop,
Its waters flow and never stop,
And in this laughing, living sea
That takes and gives so generously
We find the way to *life* and *living*
Is not in *keeping,* but in *giving!*

Yes, there are *two Palestinian seas*
And mankind is fashioned after these!

The Windows of Gold
and the Kingdom of God

There is a legend that has often been told
Of the boy who searched for the windows of gold,
The beautiful windows he saw far away
When he looked in the valley at sunrise each day,
And he yearned to go down to the valley below
But he lived on a mountain that was covered with snow
And he knew it would be a difficult trek,
But that was a journey he wanted to make,
So he planned by day and he dreamed by night
Of how he could reach *the great shining light* . . .
And one golden morning when dawn broke through
And the valley sparkled with diamonds of dew
He started to climb down the mountainside
With *the windows of gold* as his goal and his guide . . .
He traveled all day and, weary and worn,
With bleeding feet and clothes that were torn
He entered the peaceful valley town
Just as the *golden sun went down* . . .
But he seemed to have lost his *"guiding light,"*
The windows were dark that had once been bright,
And hungry and tired and lonely and cold
He cried, *"Won't you show me the windows of gold?"*
And a kind hand touched him and said, "Behold!
High on the mountain are the windows of gold" . . .
For the sun going down in a great golden ball
Had burnished the windows of his cabin so small,
And *the Kingdom of God* with its great shining light,
Like the *golden windows* that shone so bright,
Is not a far distant place, somewhere,
It's as close to you as a silent prayer—
And your search for God will end and begin
When you look for *Him* and *find Him within.*

He carried the cross to Calvary,
Carried its burden for you and me,
There on the cross He was crucified
And, because He suffered and bled and died,
We know that whatever *"our cross"* may be,
It leads to *God* and *Eternity* . . .
For who can hope for a "crown of stars"
Unless it is earned with suffering and scars,
For how could we face the living Lord
And rightfully claim His promised reward
If we have not carried our cross of care
And tasted the cup of bitter despair . . .
Let those who yearn for the pleasures of life,
And long to escape all suffering and strife,
Rush recklessly on to an "empty goal"
With never a thought of the spirit and soul . . .
But if you are searching to find the way
To life everlasting and eternal day—
With Faith in your heart take the path He trod,
For the *way of the cross* is the *way to God.*

A Mother's love is something
   that no one can explain,
It is made of deep devotion
   and of sacrifice and pain,
It is endless and unselfish
   and enduring come what may
For nothing can destroy it
   or take that love away . . .
It is patient and forgiving
   when all others are forsaking,
And it never fails or falters
   even though the heart is breaking . . .
It believes beyond believing
   when the world around condemns,
And it glows with all the beauty
   of the rarest, brightest gems . . .
It is far beyond defining,
   it defies all explanation,
And it still remains a secret
   like the mysteries of creation . . .
A many splendored miracle
   man cannot understand
And another wondrous evidence
   of God's tender guiding hand.

Where There Is Love

Where there is love
  the heart is light,
Where there is love
  the day is bright,
Where there is love
  there is a song
To help when things
  are going wrong,
Where there is love
  there is a smile
To make all things
  seem more worthwhile,
Where there is love
  there's quiet peace,
A tranquil place
  where turmoils cease—
Love changes darkness
  into light
And makes the heart
  take "wingless flight"
Oh, blest are they
  who walk in love,
They also walk
  with God above—
And when man walks
  with God again,
There shall be *peace*
  on earth for *men.*

"The Heavens Declare the Glory of God"

You ask me how I know it's true
That there is a living God—
A God who rules the universe,
The sky . . . the sea . . . the sod;
A God who holds all creatures
In the hollow of His hand;
A God who put Infinity
In one tiny grain of sand;
A God who made the seasons—
Winter, Summer, Fall and Spring,
And put His flawless rhythm
Into each created thing;
A God who hangs the sun out
Slowly with the break of day,
And gently takes the stars in
And puts the night away;
A God whose mighty handiwork
Defies the skill of man,
For no architect can alter
God's *Perfect Master Plan*—
What better answers are there
To prove His Holy Being
Than the wonders all around us
That are ours just for the seeing.

Give Lavishly! Live Abundantly!

The more you give,
    the more you get—
The more you laugh,
    the less you fret—
The more you do
    unselfishly,
The more you live
    abundantly . . .
The more of everything
    you share,
The more you'll always
    have to spare—
The more you love,
    the more you'll find
That life is good
    and friends are kind . . .
For only *what*
    we give away,
Enriches us
    from *day* to *day*.

Refuse to be discouraged,
Refuse to be distressed,
For when we are despondent
Our life cannot be blessed—
For doubt and fear and worry
Close the door to *faith* and *prayer*,
For there's no room for blessings
When we're lost in deep despair—
So remember when you're troubled
With uncertainty and doubt
It is best to tell *Our Father*
What our fear is all about—
For unless we seek His guidance
When troubled times arise
We are bound to make decisions
That are twisted and unwise—
But when we view our problems
Through the eyes of God above,
Misfortunes turn to blessings
And hatred turns to love.

Strangers Are Friends We Haven't Met

God knows *no strangers,*
He loves us all,
The poor, the rich,
The great, the small . . .
He is a friend
Who is always there
To share our troubles
And lessen our care . . .
No one is a stranger
In God's sight,
For *God is Love*
And in *His Light*
May we, too, try
In our small way
To make *new friends*
Fom day to day . . .
So pass no stranger
With an unseeing eye,
For God may be sending
A new friend by.

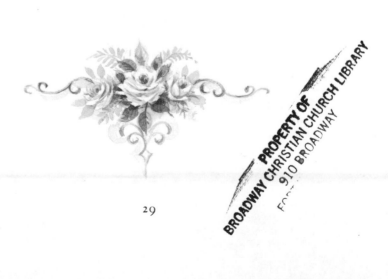

How Great the Yield
from
a Fertile Field

The farmer ploughs through
     the fields of green
And the blade of the plough
     is sharp and keen,
But the seed must be sown
     to bring forth grain,
For nothing is born
     without suffering and pain—
And God never ploughs
     in the soul of man
Without intention
     and purpose and plan,
So whenever you feel
     the plough's sharp blade
Let not your heart
     be sorely afraid
For, like the farmer,
     God chooses a field
From which He expects
     an excellent yield—
So rejoice though your heart
     is broken in two,
God seeks to bring forth
     a rich harvest in you.

He Asks So Little
and
Gives So Much

What must I do
    to insure peace of mind?
Is the answer I'm seeking,
    too hard to find?
How can I know
    what God wants me to be?
How can I tell
    what's expected of me?
Where can I go
    for guidance and aid
To help me correct
    the errors I've made?
The answer is found
    in doing *three things*
And great is the gladness
    that doing them brings . . .
"Do justice"—"Love kindness"—
    "Walk humbly with God"—
For with these *three things*
    as your "rule and your rod"
All things worth having
    are yours to achieve
If you follow God's words
    and have *faith* to *believe!*

Somebody Cares

Somebody cares and always will,
The world forgets but God loves you still,
You cannot go beyond His Love
No matter what you're guilty of—
For God forgives until the end,
He is your faithful, loyal friend,
And though you try to hide your face
There is no shelter any place
That can escape His watchful eye,
For on the earth and in the sky
He's ever present and *always there*
To take you in His tender care
And bind the wounds and mend the breaks
When all the world around forsakes . . .
Somebody cares and *loves you still*
And *God* is *the Someone* who always will.

The Magic of Love

Love is like *magic*
And it always will be,
For love still remains
Life's sweet mystery!

Love works in ways
That are wondrous and strange
And there's *nothing in life*
That *love cannot change!*

Love can transform
The most commonplace
Into beauty and splendor
And sweetness and grace!

Love is unselfish,
Understanding and kind,
For it sees with its *heart*
And not with its mind!

Love is the answer
That everyone seeks—
Love is the language
That every heart speaks—

Love can't be bought,
It is priceless and free,
Love, like pure *magic*,
Is a *sweet mystery!*

"Unless you become as children"
    And love Me as they do,
You cannot enter My Kingdom,
    For the door is closed to you . . .
For Faith is the key to heaven
    And only God's children hold
The key that opens the gateway
    To that beautiful City of Gold . . .
For only a child yet unblemished
    By the doctrines and theories of man
Is content to Trust and Love Jesus
    Without understanding His Plan.

"Heart Gifts"

It's not the things that can be bought
    that are life's richest treasure,
It's just the little "heart gifts"
    that money cannot measure . . .
A cheerful smile, a friendly word,
    a sympathetic nod
Are priceless little treasures
    from the storehouse of our God . . .
They are the things that can't be bought
    with silver or with gold,
For thoughtfulness and kindness
    and love are never sold . . .
They are the priceless things in life
    for which no one can pay,
And the giver finds rich recompense
    in *giving them away*.

"He Was One of Us"

He was born as little children are
and lived as children do,
So remember that the Saviour
was once a child like you,
And remember that He lived on earth
in the midst of sinful men,
And the problems of the present
existed even then;
He was ridiculed and laughed at
in the same heartbreaking way
That we who fight for justice
are ridiculed today;
He was tempted . . . He was hungry . . .
He was lonely . . . He was sad . . .
There's no sorrowful experience
that the Saviour has not had;
And in the end He was betrayed
and even crucified,
For He was truly "One Of Us"—
He lived on earth and died;
So do not heed the skeptics
who are often heard to say:
"What Does God Up In Heaven
Know Of Things We Face Today" . . .
For, our Father up in heaven
is very much aware
Of our failures and shortcomings
and the burdens that we bear;
So whenever you are troubled
put your problems in God's Hand
For He has faced all problems
and He Will Understand.

Great Faith That Smiles
Is Born of Great Trials

It's easy to say, *"In God we trust"*
When life is radiant and fair,
But the test of faith is only found
When there are burdens to bear—
For our claim to faith in the "sunshine"
Is really *no faith at all*
For when roads are smooth and days are bright
Our need for God is so small,
And no one discovers the fullness
Or the greatness of God's love
Unless he has walked in the "darkness"
With only a *light* from *Above*—
For the faith to endure whatever comes
Is born of sorrow and trials,
And strengthened only by discipline
And nurtured by self-denials—
So be not disheartened by troubles,
For trials are the "building blocks"
On which to erect a *fortress* of *faith*
Secure on God's "ageless rocks."

37

What More Can You Ask

God's love endureth forever—
What a wonderful thing to know
When the tides of life run against you
And your spirit is downcast and low . . .

God's kindness is ever around you,
Always ready to freely impart
Strength to your faltering spirit,
Cheer to your lonely heart . . .

God's presence is ever beside you,
As near as the reach of your hand,
You have but to tell Him your troubles,
There is nothing He won't understand . . .

And knowing God's love is unfailing,
And His mercy unending and great,
You have but to trust in His promise—
"God comes not too soon nor too late" . . .

So wait with a heart that is patient
For the goodness of God to prevail—
For never do prayers go unanswered,
And His mercy and love never fail.

When I Must Leave You

When I must leave you
  for a little while,
Please do not grieve
  and shed wild tears
And hug your sorrow
  to you through the years,
But start out bravely
  with a gallant smile;
And for my sake
  and in my name
Live on and do
  all things the same,
Feed not your loneliness
  on empty days,
But fill each waking hour
  in useful ways,
Reach out your hand
  in comfort and in cheer
And I in turn will comfort you
  and hold you near;
And never, never
  be afraid to die,
For I am waiting
  for you in the sky!

A Thankful Heart

Take nothing for granted,
  for whenever you do
The "joy of enjoying"
  is lessened for you—
For we rob our own lives
  much more than we know
When we fail to respond
  or in any way show
Our thanks for the blessings
  that daily are ours . . .
The warmth of the sun,
  the fragrance of flowers,
The beauty of twilight,
  the freshness of dawn,
The coolness of dew
  on a green velvet lawn,
The kind little deeds
  so thoughtfully done,
The favors of friends
  and the love that someone
Unselfishly gives us
  in a myriad of ways,
Expecting no payment
  and no words of praise—
Oh, great is our loss
  when we no longer find
A thankful response
  to things of this kind,
For the *joy* of *enjoying*
  and the *fullness* of *living*
Are found in the heart
  that is filled with *thanksgiving*.

Burdens Are Things
God Turns Into Wings

"Oh for the wings of a bird," we cry,
To carry us off to an untroubled sky
Where we can dwell untouched by care
And always be free as a bird in the air—
But there is a legend that's very old,
Not often heard and seldom told,
That once all birds were wingless, too,
Unable to soar through the skies of blue—
For, while their plumage was beautifully bright
And their chirping songs were liltingly light,
They, too, were powerless to fly
Until one day when the Lord came by
And laid at the feet of the singing birds
Gossamer wings as He spoke these words:
"Come take these burdens, so heavy now,
But if you bear them you'll learn somehow
That as you wear them they'll grow light
And soon you can lift yourself into flight"—
So folding the wings beneath their hearts,
And after endless failures and starts,
They lifted themselves and found with delight
The wings that were heavy had grown so light—
So let us, too, listen to God's wise words,
For we are much like the "wingless birds,"
And if we would shoulder our daily trials
And learn to wear them with sunny smiles
We'd find they were wings that God had sent
To lift us above our heart's discontent—
For *the wings* that *lift* us out of despair
Are made by God from the weight of care,
So whenever you cry for "the wings of a bird"
Remember this little legend you've heard
And let God give you a heart that sings
As He turns your burdens to "silver wings."

Before You Can Dry Another's Tears— You Too Must Weep!

Let me not live a life that's free
From *"the things"* that draw me close to *thee*—
For how can I ever hope to heal
The wounds of others I do not feel—
If my eyes are dry and I never weep,
How do I know when the hurt is deep—
If my heart is cold and it never bleeds,
How can I tell what my brother needs—
For when ears are deaf to the beggar's plea
And we close our eyes and refuse to see,
And we steel our hearts and harden our mind,
And we count it a weakness whenever we're kind,
We are no longer following *the Father's Way*
Or seeking His guidance from day to day—
For, without "crosses to carry" and "burdens to bear,"
We dance through a life that is frothy and fair,
And "chasing the rainbow" we have no desire
For "roads that are rough" and "realms that are higher"—
So spare me no heartache or sorrow, dear Lord,
For the heart that is hurt reaps the richest reward,
And God enters the heart that is broken with sorrow
As he opens the door to a *brighter tomorrow*,
For only through tears can we recognize
The suffering that lies in another's eyes.

Ideals Are Like Stars

In this world of casual carelessness
    it's discouraging to try
To keep our morals and standards
    and our *ideals high* . . .
We are ridiculed and laughed at
    by the smart sophisticate
Who proclaims in brittle banter
    that such things are out of date . . .
But no life is worth the living
    unless it's built on truth,
And we lay our life's foundation
    in the golden years of youth . . .
So allow no one to stop you
    or hinder you from laying
A firm and strong foundation
    made of *faith* and *love* and *praying* . . .
And remember that *ideals*
    are like *stars up in the sky,*
You can never really reach them,
    hanging in the heavens high . . .
But like the mighty mariner
    who sailed the storm-tossed sea,
And used *the stars to chart his course*
    with skill and certainty,
You too can *chart your course in life*
    with *high ideals* and *love,*
For *high ideals* are like the *stars*
    that light the sky above . . .
You cannot ever reach them,
    but *lift your heart up high*
And your *life will be as shining*
    as *the stars up in the sky.*

"Seek Ye First the Kingdom of God"

Life is a mixture
     of sunshine and rain,
Good things and bad things,
     pleasure and pain,
We can't have all sunshine,
     but it's certainly true
There is never a cloud
     the sun doesn't shine through . . .
So always remember
     that whatever betide you
The power of God
     is always beside you,
And if friends disappoint you
     and plans go astray
And nothing works out
     in just the right way,
And you feel you have failed
     in achieving your goal,
And that life wrongly placed you
     in an unfitting role,

Take heart and "stand tall"
  and think who you are,
For God is your Father
  and no one can bar
Or keep you from reaching
  your desired success,
Or withhold the joy
  that is yours to possess . . .
For with God on your side
  it matters not who
Is working to keep
  life's good things from you,
For you need nothing more
  than God's guidance and love
To insure you the things
  that you're most worthy of . . .
So trust in His wisdom
  and follow His ways,
And be not concerned
  with the world's empty praise,
But seek *first His Kingdom*
  and you will possess
The world's greatest riches
  which is true happiness.

In Times Like These

We read the headlines daily
        and listen to the news,
We shake our heads despairingly
        and glumly sing the blues,
We are restless and dissatisfied
        and we do not feel secure,
We are vaguely discontented
        with the things we must endure . . .
This violent age we live in
        is filled with nameless fears
As we listen to the newscasts
        that come daily to our ears,
And we view the threatening future
        with sad sobriety
As we're surrounded daily
        by increased anxiety . . .
How can we find security
        or stand on solid ground
When there's violence and dissension
        and confusion all around;
Where can we go for refuge
        from the rising tides of hate,

Where can we find a haven
        to escape this shameful fate . . .
So instead of reading headlines
        that disturb the heart and mind,
Let us open up the *Bible*
        and in doing so we'll find
That this age is no different
        from the millions gone before,
But in every hour of crisis
        God has opened up a door
For all who seek His guidance
        and trust His all-wise plan,
For God provides protection
        beyond that devised by man . . .
And we learn that each *tomorrow*
        is not ours to understand,
But lies safely in the keeping
        of the great Creator's Hand,
And to have the steadfast knowledge
        that *we never walk alone*
And to rest in the assurance
        that our *every need is known*
Will help dispel our worries,
        our anxieties and care,
For doubt and fear are vanquished
        in *the peacefulness of prayer.*

"The Fruit of the Spirit Is Love and Peace"

There is no thinking person
Who can stand untouched today
And view the world around us
Slowly drifting to decay
Without feeling deep within him
A silent, unnamed dread
As he contemplates the future
That lies frighteningly ahead . . .
For, like watching storm clouds gather
In a dark and threatening sky,
Man knows that there is nothing
He can formulate or try
That will stop the storm from breaking
In its fury and its force,
Nor can he change or alter
The storm's destructive course,
But his anxious fears are lessened
When he calls on God above,
For he knows above the storm clouds

Is the brightness of God's love . . .
So as the *"clouds of chaos"*
Gather in man's muddled mind,
And he searches for the answer
He *alone* can never find,
Let us recognize we're facing
Problems man has never solved,
And with all our daily efforts
Life grows more and more involved,
But our future will seem brighter
And we'll meet with less resistance
If we call upon our Father
And seek Divine Assistance . . .
For the spirit can unravel
Many tangled, knotted threads
That defy the skill and power
Of the world's best hands and heads,
And our plans for growth and progress,
Of which we all have dreamed,
Cannot survive materially
Unless *our spirits* are redeemed . . .
And only through a living *faith*
Can man achieve this goal,
For safety and security
Are born within the soul.

So Swift the Way!
So Short the Day!

In this fast-moving world
    of turmoil and tension,
With problems and troubles,
    too many to mention,
Our days are so crowded
    and our hours are so few,
There's *so little time*
    and *so much to do* . . .
We are *pressured* and *pushed*
    until we are "dizzy,"
There's never a minute
    we're not "crazily busy,"
And sometimes we wonder
    as we rush through the day—
Does God really want us
    to hurry this way?
Why are we impatient
    and continually vexed,
And often bewildered,
    disturbed and perplexed?
Perhaps we're too busy
    with our own selfish seeking
To hear the dear Lord
    when He's tenderly speaking . . .

We are working so tensely
        in our self-centered way,
We've no time for listening
        to what God has to say,
And hard as we work,
        at the end of the day
We know in our hearts
        we did not "pay our way" . . .
But God in His mercy
        looks down on us all,
And though what we've done
        is so pitifully small,
He makes us feel welcome
        to kneel down and pray
For the chance to do better
        as we start a new day,
And life would be better
        if we learned to rely
On our Father in heaven
        without asking *"why"* . . .
And if we'd remember
        as we rush through the day,
"The Lord is our Shepherd
        and *He'll lead the way"* . . .
So don't rush ahead
        in reckless endeavor,
Remember *"He leadeth"*
        and *"Time is forever"!*

I Do Not Go Alone

If *Death* should beckon me
    with outstretched hand
And whisper softly
    of *"an unknown land"* . . .

I shall not be
    afraid to go,
For though the path
    I do not know . . .

I take *Death's hand*
    without a fear,
For He who safely
    brought me here . . .

Will also take me
    safely back,
And though in many
    things I lack . . .

He will not let
    me go alone
Into the *"valley*
    that's *unknown"* . . .

So I reach out
    and take *Death's hand*
And journey
    to the *"Promised Land"!*

Fulfillment

Apple blossoms bursting wide
    now beautify the tree
And make a Springtime picture
    that is beautiful to see . . .
Oh, fragrant lovely blossoms,
    you'll make a bright bouquet
If I but break your branches
    from the apple tree today . . .
But if I break your branches
    and make your beauty mine,
You'll bear no fruit in season
    when severed from the vine . . .
And when we cut ourselves away
    from guidance that's divine,
Our lives will be as fruitless
    as the branch without the vine . . .
For as the flowering branches
    depend upon the tree
To nourish and fulfill them
    till they reach futurity,
We too must be dependent
    on our Father up above,
For we are but the *branches*
    and He's *the Tree of Love.*

"Climb 'Til Your Dream Comes True"

Often your tasks will be many,
And more than you think you can do . . .
Often the road will be rugged
And the hills insurmountable, too . . .
But always remember, the hills ahead
Are never as steep as they seem,
And with Faith in your heart start upward
And climb 'til you reach your dream,
For nothing in life that is worthy
Is ever too hard to achieve
If you have the courage to try it
And you have the Faith to believe . . .
For Faith is a force that is greater
Than knowledge or power or skill
And many defeats turn to triumph
If you trust in God's wisdom and will . . .
For Faith is a mover of mountains,
There's nothing that God cannot do,
So start out today with Faith in your heart
And *"climb 'til your dream comes true"!*

"Flowers Leave Their Fragrance on the Hand That Bestows Them"

There's an old Chinese proverb
that, if practiced each day,
Would change the whole world
in a wonderful way—
Its truth is so simple,
it's so easy to do,
And it works every time
and successfully, too—
For you can't do a kindness
without a reward,
Not in silver nor gold
but in joy from the Lord—
You can't light a candle
to show others the way
Without feeling the warmth
of that bright little ray—
And you can't pluck a rose,
all fragrant with dew,
Without part of its fragrance
remaining with you.

Our Father, up in heaven,
   hear this fervent prayer:
May the people of *all nations*
   be *united* in *thy care*,
For earth's peace and man's salvation
   can come only by thy grace
And not through bombs and missiles
   and our quest for outer space . . .
For until all men recognize
   that *"the battle is the Lord's"*
And peace on earth cannot be won
   with strategy and swords,
We will go on vainly fighting,
   as we have in ages past,
Finding only empty victories
   and a peace that cannot last . . .
But we've grown so rich and mighty
   and so arrogantly strong,

We no longer ask in humbleness—
"God, show us where we're wrong" . . .
We have come to trust completely
in the power of man-made things,
Unmindful of God's mighty power
and that *He* is *"King of Kings"* . . .
We have turned our eyes away from *Him*
to go our selfish way,
And money, power and pleasure
are the gods we serve today . . .
And the good green earth God gave us
to peacefully enjoy,
Through greed and fear and hatred
we are seeking to destroy . . .
Oh, Father, up in heaven,
stir and wake our sleeping souls,
Renew our faith and lift us up
and give us higher goals,
And grant us heavenly guidance
as war threatens us again
For, more than *guided missiles,*
all the world needs *guided men.*

Prayers Can't Be Answered Unless They Are Prayed

Life without purpose
  is barren indeed—
There can't be a harvest
  unless you plant seed,
There can't be attainment
  unless there's a goal,
And man's but a robot
  unless there's a soul . . .
If we send no ships out,
  no ships will come in,
And unless there's a contest,
  nobody can win . . .
For games can't be won
  unless they are played,
And *prayers* can't be *answered*
  unless they are *prayed* . . .
So whatever is wrong
  with your life today,
You'll find a solution
  if you kneel down and pray
Not just for pleasure,
  enjoyment and health,
Not just for honors
  and prestige and wealth . . .
But *pray for a purpose*
  to *make life worth living,*
And *pray for the joy*
  of *unselfish giving,*
For *great is your gladness*
  and *rich your reward*
When you make your *life's purpose*
  the choice of the Lord.

The Prodigal Son

With riches and youth to squander
The pleasure-bent *"prodigal son"*
Left the house of his Father
In search of adventure and fun—
And in reckless and riotous living
He wasted his youth and his gold,
And stripped of his earthly possessions
He was hungry and friendless and cold—
And thus he returned to his Father
Who met him with arms open wide
And cried, "My son, you are welcome
And a banquet awaits you inside" . . .
Now this story is told to remind us
Not so much of the wandering son
But *the unchanging love of the Father*
Who gladly forgave all he'd done—
And the message contained in this story
Is a powerful, wonderful one,
For it shows *our Father in Heaven*
Waits to welcome each *prodigal son*—
And whatever have been our transgressions,
God is waiting to welcome us back
And restore us our place in His Kingdom
And give us the joy that we lack . . .
So wander no longer in darkness,
Let not your return be delayed,
For the door to God is wide open
To welcome "the sheep that have strayed."

Thanksgiving is more
    than a day in November
That students of history
    are taught to remember,
More than a date
    that we still celebrate
With turkey and dressing
    piled high on our plate . . .
For while we still offer
    the traditional prayer,
We pray out of habit
    without being aware
That the Pilgrims thanked God
    just for being alive,
For the strength that He gave them
    to endure and survive
Hunger and hardship
    that's unknown in the present
Where progress and plenty
    have made our lives pleasant . . .
And living today
    in this great and rich nation

That depends not on God
        but on mechanization,
We tend to forget
        that our forefathers came
To establish a country
        under God's name . . .
But we feel we're so strong
        we no longer need *faith*,
And it now has become
        nothing more than a wraith
Of the faith that once founded
        this powerful nation
In the name of the Maker
        and the Lord of creation . . .
Oh, teach us, dear God,
        we are all *pilgrims* still,
Subject alone
        to Your guidance and will,
And show us the way
        to purposeful living
So we may have reason
        for daily thanksgiving—
And make us once more
        a *God-fearing nation*
And not just a puppet
        of controlled automation.

The Golden Chain of Friendship

Friendship is a *golden chain,*
    The links are friends so dear,
And like a rare and precious jewel
    It's treasured more each year . . .
It's clasped together firmly
    With a love that's deep and true,
And it's rich with happy memories
    And fond recollections, too . . .
Time can't destroy its beauty
    For, as long as memory lives,
Years can't erase the pleasure
    That the joy of friendship gives . . .
For friendship is a priceless gift
    That can't be bought or sold,
But to have an understanding friend
    Is worth far more than gold . . .
And the *golden chain* of *friendship*
    Is a strong and blessed tie
Binding kindred hearts together
    As the years go passing by.

Teach Us to Live

God of love—Forgive! Forgive!
Teach us how to *truly live*,
Ask us not our race or creed,
Just take us in our hour of need,
And let us know You love us, too,
And that we are *a part of You* . . .
And someday may man realize
That all the earth, the seas and skies
Belong to God who made us all,
The rich, the poor, the great, the small,
And in the Father's Holy Sight
No man is yellow, black or white,
And *peace on earth* cannot be found
Until we *meet on common ground*
And every man becomes a *brother*
Who worships God and loves each other.

My Thanks!

People everywhere in life
    from every walk and station,
From every town and city
    and every state and nation
Have given me so many things
    intangible and dear,
I couldn't begin to count them all
    or even make them clear . . .
I only know I owe so much
    to people everywhere
And when I put my thoughts in verse
    it's just a way to share
The musings of a thankful heart,
    a heart much like your own,
For nothing that I think or write
    is mine and mine alone . . .
So if you found some beauty
    in any word or line,
It's just "Your Soul's Reflection
    in Proximity with Mine."